Introduction

This exam preparation book is just that, a preparation book. ... ... .e prep exam within the book will not guarantee a 'pass' on the exam. This book will provide you with an understanding of how the exam will be presented with similar focus on questions that may be presented to you on the actual exam.

The questions and scenarios within this book are not and will not be the questions you are asked on your exam.

The questions and scenarios are based on the publicly available information from the most current body of knowledge and blueprints for ease of understanding and to supplement your preparation.

This book outlines and walks you through one recommended way of preparing for your exam.

Exam Taking Tips

The primary essence of dissecting any exam question is to understand the question being asked.

What is 'it' that the question is asking you?

You have to understand what the question is asking before you can correctly answer the question.

Review and understand the six domains within the body of knowledge, along with each sub domain.

Knowing the domains and their objectives will assist you in being able to recall the correct answer for the question.

This book will assist you in determining what the question is asking you to answer.

Most questions on the exam have one or multiple terms presented to you. An example of a term may be 'Accountability.' Knowing what that definition is and where in the domain(s) it is relevant, will help you determine what the correct answer, if the question is asking you about 'Accountability.'

An example question (bonus question for you, the reader) may be:

An organization that suffers a cyber event may be investigated to determine if they had the appropriate policies and procedures in place, along with documented training for their workforce. If the organization had those correct controls in place, this organization is able to prove that they have?

    A. Consumer Trust
    B. Compliance
    C. Accountability
    D. Responsibility

The best, correct answer would be C. Accountability. Accountable organizations will be able to show tangible evidence that they have executed both their due care and due diligence as it relates to policy development, implementation, dissemination, training, and follow-up actions ensuring that their workforce is able to apply and comply with those policies and procedures. Consumer trust (Answer A) is a by-product of being accountable, as is Compliance (Answer B). The organization is being responsible (Answer D) by being accountable. Without being accountable, the organization would not have trust. The organization would more than likely not be compliant, nor would they be responsible in protecting their data.

These types of questions, with that thought process, is highly likely to be presented to you on your exam.

The exam is multiple choice and has numerous scenario-based questions. You have 2 hours and 30 minutes to complete the 90-question exam.

If possible, read the questions twice to help you truly understand the question being asked.

If you read the question and know the answer before you look below to the presented answers, trust that intuition. Look at the presented answers to confirm the correct answer.

If your answer is not presented in the answers, look for a similar answer. That 'similar' answer may be your correct answer.

If neither of those answers are presented, re-read the question. Look for the key 'term' and see if there is a word, such as 'any' or 'all' or if the question is asking you for 'what is NOT' a part of the term or question. Those key words will help you identify possible distracting, presented answers and lead you to eliminate those from the equation of possible questions.

You will then have two good or best answers to select from once you have completed that process.

Reflect on the definitions and terms that you have studied along with your experience to decipher the correct response. Mark that question and move on to the next question.

Learn the terms and definitions, please!

Utilize those in your day-to-day responsibilities from the point you start preparing for your exam. That will reinforce the terms, their definitions and potentially also prepare you for your future exams.

FINAL PREP

The first time you read the exam question is to train your mind to quickly reflect on the key words you read and what is being asked.

Reading the question, a second time will highlight those key words and begin to clarify what the question is really asking you to answer.

Reflect on those key words. Terms. Definitions.

Ask yourself what the question is asking you to know.

The first five questions of this book will start you on that process of asking you to read the question twice.

After that, highlight the key words of the question.

Finally, ask yourself what the question is asking you to know.

Review the questions and choose the correct answer.

Remember, you can flag a question and come back to review it at the end. Do not get frustrated if you don't know the answer.

Don't spend too much time on one particular question. If you are unsure of the answer, flag it, and move on to the next and review ALL flagged items at the end.

Do NOT leave any questions blank or unanswered.

Take your time, prepare as best you can, reference as many resources that you need to feel comfortable and prepared to take the exam.

Now, let's get started with your CIPM: FOCUSED PREPARATION 2022 and thank you for purchasing this book!

You can also find in our library the CIPP/US: FOCUSED PREPARATION 2022; the CIPP/E: FOCUSED PREPARATION 2022; the HCISPP: FOCUSED PREPARATION; the CDPSE: FOCUSED PREPARATION prep exam books along with the INCIDENT RESPONSE PLANNING: FOCUSED

PREPARATION; the CYBER TABLETOP EXERCISES: FOCUSED PREPARATION, Templates and Scenarios for your use in proactive preparation for handling cyber incidents.

If you have any questions, please feel free to contact us at timothy@stormyconsulting.com.

Now, let's get to it!

Question 1.

One of the goals that is not a Privacy Program Manager role is to?

One of the _goals_ that is _not_ a Privacy Program Manager _role_ is to?

Key words: Goals; NOT, Role

Questions to ask yourself – What are the roles of the PPM?

Which one of the answers below is not one of those roles or their goals?

Answers:
A. To identify their supply chain's privacy risks.
B. To identify their organizations, employees, patient's risks.
C. To identify current state of policies, procedures, and any supporting documentation.
D. Promote consumer trust.

Question 2.

Which of the following is not a reason organization are becoming compliant with global privacy regulations?

Which of the following reason is *not* a reason organization are becoming <u>compliant</u> with global privacy regulations?

Key words: NOT, Compliant

Questions to ask yourself – What are the reasons organizations are becoming compliant with global privacy regulations?

Which one of the answers below is not one of those reasons?

Answers:

A. Brand Name Protection
B. Reputation Protection
C. GDPR
D. U.S. Federal Privacy Law

Question 3.

Privacy program managers are charged with the protection and appropriate use of?

Privacy program managers <u>are charged</u> with the <u>protection</u> and <u>appropriate use</u> of?

Key words: are charged; protection; appropriate use

Questions to ask yourself – What or why are Privacy Program Managers at your organization? What are they responsible for? What or where is their focus?

Answers:

A. Private Information
B. Personal Information
C. Public Information
D. Social Information

Question 4.

Which of the following groups are not a priority group for the development of your privacy policies and procedures within your organization?

Which of the following groups are <u>not</u> a priority group for the <u>development</u> of your privacy <u>policies</u> and <u>procedures</u> <u>within</u> your organization?

Key words: NOT; development (hasn't been done, being built – SDLC or PbD; policies and procedures; within (internal – not external)

Questions to ask yourself – What groups develop privacy policies and procedures within your organization?   Which of the answers below is not one of those groups?

Answers:

A. Human Resources
B. Legal
C. Business Development
D. External Audit

Question 5.

The privacy vision should align with?

The privacy vision should align with?

Key words: privacy vision; align

Questions to ask yourself – What is a privacy vision? (know the definition); Where and when is the privacy vision created? What is the reason the vision is being created?

Answers:

A. Consumer Objectives
B. Business Objectives
C. Vendor Objectives
D. Contract Objectives

That concludes the trial of having the question posed to you twice, highlighting the key words and questions to ask yourself.

There may be a few more of these scattered throughout the answers in the rear of the book to keep reminding you to practice this test taking recommendation.

Question 6.

Your organization is implementing a new process that may collect consumer's information. The process is complete and ready for a final review before being launched into production. During the review, it is determined that the new process lacks the ability to audit the privacy controls for regulatory compliance. What was not included in the design?

Answers:

A. Proactive
B. Embedded privacy controls
C. Respect for users
D. Privacy by Design

Question 7.

Upon request, a detailed record of processing must be shared with the?

Answers:

A. Data Protection Officer
B. Data Protection Authority
C. Chief Information Officer
D. Chief Information Security Officer

Question 8.

Your medical staff has access to all EMRs. Each staff member is trained frequently on proper handling, access, and protecting of sensitive data. If one of your medical practitioners is unable to access an EMR, and is authorized to access it, which basic security principle has been applied?

Answers:

A. Role-Based Access
B. Segregation of duties
C. Least privilege
D. Need-to-know access

Question 9.

While your organization is assessing a potential vendor, one statement within the vendor policy may require a review of?

Answers:

A. Privacy Policy
B. Vendor Management
C. Location of data
D. Employees

Question 10.

Your organization has secured funding for a new privacy training initiative. Which of the following may not be one of the training methods you would implement?

Answers:

A. Classroom
B. Online
C. Workshops
D. Testing

Question 11.

The CFO and CHR of a healthcare organization are looking to you, the privacy program manager, to provide them with a performance measurement of the privacy program. Which of the following would you not utilize in creating that?

Answers:

A. Tracking
B. Identifying
C. Defining
D. Analyzing

Question 12.

Who needs to appreciate the benefits and risks associated with the collection and use of personal information?

Answers:

A. Privacy
B. Privacy Professional
C. Privacy Program Manager
D. Privacy Officer

Question 13.

A California, U.S. based organization receives its first subject access request (SAR). The privacy program manager is alerted to receipt of the request in a timely fashion. What will the program manager reference, that was developed in the establishment of the privacy program, that will assist in determining where the SAR's information resides?

Answers:

A. Data Classification Policy
B. Privacy Program Scope
C. Regulatory Map
D. Data Inventory

Question 14.

The GDPR, the CCPA, GLBA and other privacy regulatory laws have different terminology and requirements as it relates to 'reasonable security procedures and practices." The word, "adequate" or "appropriate technical and organizational measures' – this is the 'security principle'. Where might you not reference for these types of controls and standards?

Answers:

A. Internet Security's Critical Security Controls
B. ISO/IEC 27002
C. NIST SP 800-53rev4
D. ISO/IEC 27006

Question 15.

An organizations privacy program maturity level is based on how established the program is functioning in multiple areas. Departments are following and adhering to processes and procedures for most functions. What level of maturity is the organization at?

Answers:

A. Repeatable
B. Defined
C. Ad Hoc
D. Managed

Question 16.

An organizations privacy program maturity level is based on how established the program is functioning in multiple areas. Generally, if your privacy program has recently been created where you are still evaluating and inventorying what the organization has and does not have in place for policies, processes and procedures, the privacy program maturity level is at this stage?

Answers:

A. Repeatable
B. Defined
C. Ad Hoc
D. Managed

Question 17.

Key stakeholders make decisions pertaining your organizations privacy program. The record of these decisions serves as the privacy program's?

Answers:

A. Governance
B. Risk Assessment
C. Due Care
D. Due Diligence

Question 18.

Your customer's information and their rights to control what and who collects their information, where their information is shared are privacy rights. What overlap is there with information security that relates to accuracy of information?

Answers:

A. Availability
B. Confidentiality
C. Integrity
D. Accountability

Question 19.

As privacy laws and regulations continue to expand and change, complying and monitoring with those changes is critical for the organization's privacy program success. What is one solution that provides organizations with updated changes, monitoring and auditing performances of their processes and procedures?

Answers:

A. Internal Audit
B. Second-party Audit
C. Third-party Audit
D. Third-party Privacy Compliance Platform and Tools

Question 20.

Prior to a new service or system being implemented, this type of action is required to be conducted?

Answers:

A. Data Privacy Impact Assessment
B. Privacy Impact Assessment
C. Privacy Assessment
D. Risk Assessment

Question 21.

Your organization has been alerted to a data breach within one of your vendors. During the DPA investigation, procurement has been summoned for questioning. What may be the topic of discussion?

Answers:

A. Communications Language
B. Processor responsibilities
C. GDPR Compliance
D. Internal audit results

Question 22.

Your organization is capturing and documenting where and what information is flowing, both internally and externally. What is this type of exercise?

Answers:

A. Regulatory Map
B. Legal Map
C. Data Inventory Map
D. Data Map

Question 23.

Your organization is conducting processor assessments. Which privacy domain houses this action item?

Answers:

A. Measure
B. Improve
C. Evaluate
D. Support

Question 24.

HR is reviewing candidate's resumes and background information based on an open job posting. What is one risk area that you, as the Privacy Program Manager, should work with Legal and HR on, as it relates to the background information gathered?

Answers:

A. Data Retention
B. Data Policies
C. Information
D. Training

Question 25.

Which of the following orders are the correct order as it relates to data incidents plans?

Answers:

A. Planning, Preparing, Handling, Reporting
B. Planning, Investigating, Handling, Reporting
C. Preparing, Reporting, Investigating, Recovering
D. Preparing, Investigating, Recovering, Reporting

Question 26.

Your customer's information and their rights to control what and who collects their information, where their information is shared are privacy rights. What overlap is there with information security that relates to access of information?

Answers:

A. Availability
B. Confidentiality
C. Integrity
D. Accountability

Question 27.

Your medical staff has access to all EMRs. Each staff member is trained frequently on proper handling, access, and protecting of sensitive data. If one of your medical practitioners accesses an EMR in which they did not and will not provide care to, which basic security principle has been violated?

Answers:

A. Role-Based Access
B. Segregation of duties
C. Least privilege
D. Need-to-know access

Question 28.

Your PIA identified a risk that you, as the privacy program manager, must address to bridge a gap within your privacy training and awareness program. You present the findings and the costs associated with the mitigating activity to your leadership. They reject your request. What should you have presented to your leadership to support your request?

Answers:

A. Business Case
B. Return-on-Investment
C. Qualitative benefits
D. Annual loss expectancy (ALE)

Question 29.

A financial institution has completed their regulatory mapping exercise and determined and created their data retention policy. The institution has adopted two possible standards for destroying the data, which are degaussing and shredding. What is another way to destroy the data electronically?

Answers:

A. Melt
B. Burn
C. Erase
D. Overwrite

Question 30.

Your organization has suffered a data breach. You have initiated the incident response plan and are preparing for an external communication. Your marketing and social media team is made aware that an employee has posted a statement onto their personal social media platform. What didn't the organization do, based on the information provided?

Answers:

A. Implement a training program
B. Conduct training
C. Coordinate both internal and external communications
D. Notify customers

Question 31.

Your organization has accepted your proposed privacy vision. In order to continue developing your privacy program, which is your next step?

Answers:

A. Develop the privacy team
B. Develop the privacy program strategy
C. Develop the mission statement
D. Develop the scope of the privacy program

Question 32.

After completing the framework, which step is next in the development of the privacy program?

Answers:

A. Develop the privacy team
B. Develop the privacy program strategy
C. Develop the mission statement
D. Develop the scope of the privacy program

Question 33.

Which of the following tactics are used to identify your privacy program scope?

Answers:

A. Identify where business data is collected
B. Identify where data is collected
C. Identity where personal information is collected
D. Identify global data protection laws

Question 34.

Your organization has implemented information security practices. Which privacy domain houses this action item?

Answers:

A. Measure
B. Improve
C. Evaluate
D. Support

Question 35.

Your workforce is one of the key contributors to causing a data incident. What is one of the first things you need to determine to address this risk?

Answers:

A. Secure Funding
B. Train the workforce
C. Develop a business case
D. Workforce behavioral review

Question 36.

HR is reviewing candidate's resumes and background information based on an open job posting. What is one risk area that you, as the Privacy Program Manager, should work focus on, as it relates to the vendor gathering the background information requested?

Answers:

A. Procurement
B. Vendor Assessment
C. Information Risk
D. Communications

Question 37.

Your organization is implementing a new process that may collect consumer's information. Throughout the SDLC process, it is also determined that the consumer's information may be shared or aggregated throughout the life cycle of the information. In order to determine if a privacy impact assessment (PIA) is needed, you must conduct a?

Answers:

A. Data Privacy Impact Assessment
B. Information risk assessment
C. Privacy-enabling technology
D. Privacy threshold analysis

Question 38.

An insurance company is informed by an agent that they may have compromised personal information of their clients. What information security controls will be potentially implemented?

Answers:

A. Preventative
B. Detective
C. Corrective
D. Recovery

Question 39.

A U.S. based financial institution is required to provide customers a privacy notice annually that provides clear notice of the customer's right with respects to opt-outs. What regulation requires this?

Answers:

A. GDPR
B. LGDP
C. PIPEDA
D. GLBA

Question 40.

The stakeholders of a genetic organization have developed and are presenting their business case for a privacy program update, to include protective controls ensuring both the information security and privacy programs are united and overlapping. As part of this presentation, the quantified annual loss expectancy for a particular privacy control is $120,000 for complete development, implementation and monitoring of the control. While presenting, the question was posed to the presenter on, 'If the control is not implemented, what will be the cost to the organization?" The projected impact to the organization would be less than the actual control being implemented. What would this example be called?

Answers:

A. Qualitative model
B. Single loss expectancy
C. Return on investment (ROI)
D. Acceptable risk

Question 41.

An organizations privacy program maturity level is based on how established the program is functioning in multiple areas. The privacy program has been in place for multiple years and has been extremely successful in providing metrics and efficiencies for your organization. What level of maturity is the organization at?

Answers:

A. Repeatable
B. Defined
C. Ad Hoc
D. Managed

Question 42.

Your medical staff has access to all EMRs. Each staff member is trained frequently on proper handling, access, and protecting of sensitive data. If one of your medical practitioners accesses an EMR in which they are providing care to, which basic security principle has been followed?

Answers:

A. Role-Based Access
B. Segregation of duties
C. Least privilege
D. Need-to-know access

Question 43.

As technology infrastructure is procured, implemented, and secured, which of the following security controls are most integrated with IT?

Answers:

A. Physical Security
B. HR Security
C. Ethics and Integrity
D. Employees

Question 44.

Principles and standards, laws, regulations and programs are two categories that a privacy framework may be designed from. What is another category that can be referenced to create a privacy framework?

Answers:

A. Privacy Program Management
B. Privacy Program Strategy
C. Privacy Program Vision
D. Privacy by Default

Question 45.

Within the U.S., which federal law addresses money laundering?

Answers:

A. U.S. Federal Financial Law
B. Federal Trade Commission Act
C. Fair and Accurate Credit Transactions Act
D. Financial Modernization Act

Question 46.

Your organization must share personal information to a country outside of the EEA and EU. You individually tailor the contract your company's needs and obtain the required supervisory authority's authorization. What type of cross-border transfer rule are you using?

Answers:

A. BCR
B. SCC
C. Codes of Conduct
D. Ad hoc contractual clause

Question 47.

A global organization located in numerous countries would be best to implement this type of governance model?

Answers:

A. Centralized
B. Distributed
C. Hybrid
D. External

Question 48.

If your leadership is not supporting nor funding your privacy program management, one way to gain their support is to share what a potential privacy breach would cost the organizations. This would be an example of?

Answers:

A. Metrics
B. Quantitative Model
C. Qualitative Model
D. Return on Investment (ROI)

Question 49.

What must an efficient and successful privacy program be built with?

Answers:

A. Data Map
B. Regulatory Map
C. Compliance Map
D. Comprehensive View

Question 50.

Your organization completed the data inventory exercise. Who in your organization determines what classifications of information are arranged into those categories?

Answers:

A. Chief Security Officer
B. Chief Executive Officer
C. Privacy Officer
D. Human Resources

Question 51.

Your organization has implemented a privacy program and you are analyzing the data and metrics. What was your previous step?

Answers:

A. Identification of audience
B. Analysis
C. Collection
D. Selection

Question 52.

Once the policies, procedures and security controls have been assessed on your potential cloud provider, whom within your organization should approve of this type of vendor?

Answers:

A. General Counsel
B. Privacy Program Manager
C. Chief Information Security Officer
D. Chief Information Officer

Question 53.

Your organization is acquiring another organization. A part of the privacy checkpoint, your organization's processes should consist of conducting a _____ prior to the integration of the acquired organization's systems and processes.

Answers:

A. Divestiture
B. Data inventory
C. Regulatory map
D. Risk Assessment

Question 54.

The privacy program manager is preparing their performance measurement presentation. They are looking at the value of the asset being measured, ensuring to capture the possible changes or factors that may impact that value. What other consideration should the PPM take into account as they develop the presentation?

Answers:

A. Return on investment
B. Chief Financial Officer
C. Alignment
D. Integration

Question 55.

An insurance company is informed by an agent noticed that their computer screen is open, and they are certain that they had locked the screen and that they may have compromised personal information of their clients. What information security controls may be audited?

Answers:

A. Access Controls
B. Asset Management
C. Procurement
D. Training

Question 56.

You are making a purchase on an e-commerce website and you receive a notice in the middle of the page that articulates what the organization does to protect your information. You have not yet provided any personal information. What is this called?

Answers:

A. Opt-Out
B. Opt-In
C. Just-in-time-notice
D. Privacy Policy

Question 57.

An organizations privacy program maturity level is based on how established the program is functioning in multiple areas. Regular audits, assessments, guidance and communications are gathered to review and improve the overall privacy program. What level of maturity is the organization at?

Answers:

A. Repeatable
B. Defined
C. Optimized
D. Managed

Question 58.

Your customer's information and their rights to control what and who collects their information, where their information is shared are privacy rights. What overlap is there with information security that relates to accountability?

Answers:

A. Availability
B. Confidentiality
C. Integrity
D. Accountability

Question 59.

It is Monday morning and you are starting a new role. You log into your corporate email account and find an email from HR. As you read through the email, you see that you are required to complete specific privacy training. What type of control is this?

A. Special Handling
B. Data Classification
C. Technical
D. Role-Based Access

Question 60.

HR is reviewing candidate's resumes and background information based on an open job posting. What is one risk area that you, as the Privacy Program Manager, should work with HR on, as it relates to the background information gathered?

Answers:

A. Contracts
B. Procurement
C. Marketing
D. Data

Question 61.

Your organization has suffered a data breach. Your organization has implemented their incident response plan. Which privacy domain houses this action item?

Answers:

A. Measure
B. Improve
C. Evaluate
D. Support

Question 62.

Your privacy program needs to monitor changes, organizational compliance, but it doesn't need to integrate with?

Answers:

A. Legal changes
B. Cultural changes
C. Technological changes
D. Employee changes

Question 63.

Your organization has implemented a privacy program and you are preparing to present metrics captured. What was your initial step in this process?

Answers:

A. Identification of audience
B. Analysis
C. Collection
D. Selection

Question 64.

Your organization has implemented a privacy program and you are defining your data sources. What is your next step?

Answers:

A. Identification of audience
B. Analysis
C. Collection
D. Selection

Question 65.

An insurance company is informed by an agent that they may have compromised personal information of their clients. What is this called when the agent thinks the information has been compromised?

Answers:

A. Incident Detection
B. Incident Handling
C. Incident Response Plan
D. Employee Training

Question 66.

When your organization has purchased cyber liability insurance, and suffer a data breach, your incident response plan is then followed and one of the first calls would be to?

Answers:

A. Forensic Firm
B. Data Protection Authority
C. CSO
D. Breach Coach

Question 67.

Who, within your organization, would the privacy program manager not work with to better understand the organizations privacy needs?

Answers:

A. CPO
B. DPO
C. DPA
D. General Counsel

Question 68.

Of the following, which is a privacy framework that may be used for your privacy program management framework?

Answers:

A. ENISA
B. EFCC
C. CNIL
D. DPA

Question 69.

This regulation offers organizations a new framework for data protection?

Answers:

A. GDPR
B. LGDP
C. PIPEDA
D. APPI

Question 70.

As you assess your prospective vendors, what is one topic that is not a priority for you to assess?

Answers:

A. Financial
B. Geographic Location(s)
C. Privacy Framework
D. Data Inventory

Question 71.

You are making a purchase on an e-commerce website and a banner at the bottom of the page appears before you can provide your billing and shipping information. This banner articulates what the organization does to protect your information. What is this called?

Answers:

A. Opt-Out
B. Opt-In
C. Privacy Notice
D. Privacy Policy

Question 72.

What is measured via metrics associated with confidentiality, unavailability, and projected business impact assessments for downtime within an organizations business objectives?

Answers:

A. Accountability
B. Data Privacy
C. Data Protection
D. Business Resiliency

Question 73.

A California, US based organization receives its first subject access request (SAR). The privacy program manager is alerted to receipt of the request in a timely fashion. What is the first step of the organization upon receipt of the SAR?

Answers:

A. Verify Identity of Requestor
B. Review BIPA
C. Regulatory Map
D. Data Inventory

Question 74.

Which of the following are not privacy matters to consider?

Answers:

A. Geographical location
B. Global Privacy Regulations
C. Cross-border data sharing
D. Competitor's Privacy Strategy

Question 75.

What is developed to guide your organization in disseminating and adoption for your privacy program?

Answers:

A. Developing the privacy vision
B. Developing the privacy strategy
C. Developing the privacy framework
D. Developing the privacy structure

Question 76.

Within your organization, who is responsible for protecting personal information that is captured and processed?

Answers:

A. Consumer
B. Vendor
C. Patient
D. Workforce

Question 77.

What must be implemented and is the first cornerstone that builds a foundation for an effective privacy management program?

Answers:

A. Privacy Vision
B. Privacy Scope
C. Privacy Framework
D. Privacy Strategy

Question 78.

Your organization is capturing and documenting where and what information is flowing, both internally and externally. What does the end product assist your organization with?

Answers:

A. Identifies vendors
B. Identifies regulatory requirements
C. Identifies classification
D. Identifies personal information use

Question 79.

Your organization, a covered entity within the U.S., has suffered a data breach within your archived information. What policy will be looked at to determine whether or not your organization has complied with that policy?

Answers:

A. Acceptable Use
B. BYOD
C. Incident Response Plan
D. Retention

Question 80.

Your organization is structuring your privacy team. Which privacy domain houses this action item?

Answers:

A. Measure
B. Improve
C. Privacy Program Framework
D. Developing a Privacy Program

Question 81.

Under what U.S. law requires government agencies to conduct a privacy impact assessment?

Answers:

A. FISMA
B. FACTA
C. E-Commerce Act
D. E-Government Act

Question 82.

An insurance company is informed by an agent that they may have compromised personal information of their clients. What is this called?

Answers:

A. Data Breach
B. Privacy Incident
C. Cyber Security
D. Incident Response Framework

Question 83.

Who is responsible for monitoring, improving, reporting and communicating the criticality of a particular metric?

Answers:

A. Privacy Manager
B. Privacy Owner
C. Communications Leader
D. Metric owner

Question 84.

An international manufacturing company is implementing their privacy program. While they are in that process, they are conducting self-assessments, developing procedures, communicating and monitoring the program. What type of management is this called?

Answers:

A. Information Security Management System
B. Risk Management
C. Centralized Management
D. Information Management

Question 85.

Your organization has suffered a data breach. You have initiated the incident response plan and are preparing for an external communication. Which or who would be best to communicate that message externally?

Answers:

A. HR
B. Ethics and Integrity
C. Marketing Dept.
D. CEO

Question 86.

In order for you to assess a cloud provider, you must understand their?

Answers:

A. Privacy
B. Mission Statement
C. Notice
D. Policies

Question 87.

Which one of the following is not one of the most common causes of a data breach?

Answers:

A. Malicious Actors
B. Human Error
C. System Glitches
D. Vendors

Question 88.

The information security group utilizes a systematic approach to manage information risks relating to people, processes, and technologies. What is the name of this approach?

Answers:

A. Privacy Framework
B. Information Security
C. Information Privacy Management System
D. Information Security Management System

Question 89.

These guidelines apply to all media and address marketing plans?

Answers:

A. Network Advertising Initiative (NAI)
B. VeriSign
C. PCI DSS
D. DMA Guidelines for Ethical Business Practices

Question 90.

Privacy programs and their leadership may fall under multiple areas within organizations. They may fall under Legal, HR, IT, Risk, or other areas.
As your organization determines which area it may report to, the organization should take all of the following into consideration, except:

Answers:

A. Organizational structure
B. Roles and responsibilities
C. Evaluation
D. Vendor Management

Additional Questions for your review.

91. All the following are factors in determining whether an organization can craft a common solution to the privacy requirements of multiple jurisdictions EXCEPT:

A. Effective date of most restrictive law.
B. Implementation complexity.
C. Legal regulations.
D. Expense considerations.

92. Under the FCRA, if inaccurate information is discovered in a consumer's file, what is the usual time in which the credit reporting agency must examine the disputed information?

A. In a timely manner.
B. Within 30 days of notification.
C. Within 45 days of notification.
D. Within 60 days of notification.

93. Which of the following is NOT a good reason to perform a privacy audit on a supplier?

A. The vendor management team is validating the supplier as part of a regular onboarding process.
B. The finance team has concerns that their supplier is inflating their pass-through expense costs.
C. The legal team received notification of a personal data breach caused by the supplier.
D. The IT team received a notice that the supplier is changing their cloud-storage subprocessors.

94. A healthcare organization began integrating the concept of privacy into all facets of their organization, to include targeted and specialized training for handling of sensitive information, along with the adoption within the conceptual and design phases of new business processes, IT systems, contractual agreements, devices and policies. What is this concept of applying privacy solutions into early phases of development known as?

A. Pseudonymization.
B. Data minimization.
C. Privacy by design.
D. Security by design.

95. An example of media sanitization would be:

A. Installing a password on a laptop and requiring password to be changed on a scheduled basis.
B. Restricting employees' thumb drive access to locked drives provided by the organization.
C. Performing a manufacturer's reset to restore an office printer to its factory default settings.
D. Implementing a blocker to limit the ability of connected devices to access specific online sites.

96. What role would data loss prevention software have in a privacy program?

A. Prevention of all data breaches caused through human error by employees.
B. Protection from an external hacker trying to infiltrate an organization's networks.
C. Training for staff on data governance and proper data classification procedures.
D. Monitoring of certain types of personal data disclosures to outside entities.

97. When should stakeholders be identified in the development of a privacy framework?

A. After the privacy team has established its agenda.
B. After the data inventory is complete.
C. During the review of written policies.
D. During the business case development process.

98. Which of the following is NOT one of the four principles an organization should consider when aligning information privacy and information security technologies?

A. Prioritize the expense of the technology and supplement any shortfalls with alternate programs (Cost-based priority).
B. Ensure privacy, information security and development teams work together to evaluate controls (Teaming).
C. Ensure security risks are part of the privacy risk framework to include correctly implemented controls (Stay aware).
D. Prioritize risks and allocate resources accordingly so higher risk concerns are addressed first (Rank and prioritize).

99. Access to an organization's information systems should be tied to an employee's role, and therefore, determined by basic security principles for role-based access controls (RBAC). Which of the following contains the correct role-based access controls principles?

A. Least privilege, segregation of duties, need-to-know access.
B. Right-to-access, need-to-know access, segregation of duties.
C. Functional role access, segregation of duties, least privilege.
D. Segregation of duties, need-to-know access, access privilege.

100.   Where should an organization's procedures for resolving consumer complaints about privacy protection be found?

A. In the emergency response plan.
B. In memoranda from the CEO.
C. In written policies regarding privacy.
D. In the minutes of organizational board meetings.

101.   Each of the following organizations could consider developing a highly centralized privacy team structure EXCEPT:

A. Grape2Table, a small- to medium-sized enterprise sourcing fine wines direct from vineyards for its customers, with multiple offices throughout France.
B. SudsLow, a large franchise of tradespeople performing cleaning services across the United States with all executive management based in the central HQ in Ohio.
C. DiverzityCorp, an industrial conglomerate with multiple product and service lines with separate divisions based in the U.S., Brazil and China, each with its own management team.
D. Hoopdehoop, an online retail company that sells children's toys and games throughout multiple countries in the EU, through a variety of different websites, but is based in the Netherlands.

102.   What is business resiliency?

A. How quickly a business accomplishes a merger.
B. How well a business responds to and adapts after a disaster.
C. How successful a business's auditing process is.
D. How well a business rewards and retains its employees.

103.   Each of the following are actions an organization should take when developing a data retention policy EXCEPT:

A. Work with legal advisors to determine applicable legal data retention requirements.
B. Instruct processors to keep information based on approved legal requirements.
C. Estimate what business impacts are of retaining versus destroying the data.
D. Brainstorm with appropriate personnel scenarios that would require data retention.

104.   What is the value of a privacy workshop for an organization's stakeholders?

A. A workshop ensures compliance to policies at all levels of an organization.
B. A workshop ensures all stakeholders commit resources to the privacy program.
C. A workshop ensures common baseline understanding of the risks and challenges.
D. A workshop ensures there is a single privacy policy across the organization.

105.   Acme Co. wants to develop a new mobile application that will allow users to find friends by continuously tracking the locations of the devices on which the application is installed. Which one of the following should Acme Co. do before developing the application to minimize its privacy risks?

A. Determine how to communicate breach notifications.
B. Test the accuracy of the continuous location mechanism.
C. Calculate the return on investment.
D. Conduct a privacy (or data protection) impact assessment.

106.   When conducting a baseline assessment of your privacy program, you should:

A. Ensure your documentation reflects the expected future state of the program.
B. Document areas of remediation that are currently in progress.
C. Quantify the costs of existing and needed technical controls.
D. Establish a system for implementing privacy by design.

SCENARIO I
Use the following to answer questions 107-111:

Country Fresh Sundries started in the kitchen of its founder, Margaret Holmes, as she made soap following a traditional family recipe. It is a much different business today, having grown first through product placement in health and beauty retail outlets, then through a thriving catalog business. The company was slow to launch an online store, but once it did, the online business grew rapidly. Online sales now account for 65 percent of business, which is increasingly international in scope. In fact, Country Fresh is now a leading seller of luxury soaps in Europe and South America, as well as continuing its strong record of growth in the United States. Despite its rapid ascent, Country Fresh prides itself on maintaining its homey atmosphere, as symbolized by its company headquarters with a farmhouse in front of a factory in a rural region of Maine, in the U.S. The company is notably "employee friendly," allowing, for instance, employees to use their personal computers for conducting business and encouraging people to work at home to spend more time with their families.

As the incoming director of privacy, you are the company's first dedicated privacy professional. During the interview process, you found that while the people you talked to, including Shelly Holmes, CEO and daughter of the founder, and Jim Greene, vice president for operations, meant well, they did not possess a sophisticated knowledge of privacy practices and regulations and were unsure of exactly where the company stood in relation to compliance and security. Jim candidly admitted, "We know there is a lot we need to be thinking about and doing regarding privacy, but none of us know much about it. We have put some safeguards in place, but we are not even sure they are effective. We need someone to build a privacy program from the ground up."

The final interview ended after the close of business. The cleaning crew had started its nightly work. As you walked through the office, you noticed that computers had been left on at employee workstations and the only shredder you saw was marked with a sign that said, "Out of Order. Do Not Use."

You have accepted the job offer and are about to report to work on Monday. You are now on a plane headed toward your new office, considering your course of action in this position, and jotting down some notes.

107.   How can you discover where personal data resides at Country Fresh?

A. By focusing solely on emerging technologies, as they present the greatest risks.
B. By checking all public interfaces for breaches of personal data.
C. By performing a gap analysis and creating a plan to bridge those gaps.
D. By conducting a data inventory and mapping data flows.

108.   You need a master plan or roadmap to guide your choices in developing and refining Country Fresh's privacy program. What is the best action to take?

A. Adopt the privacy program mission statement as a guide to specific actions.
B. Modify industry best practices to fit the organization's needs.
C. Perform a mapping exercise that reveals where personal data resides.
D. Develop an overarching privacy program framework.

109.   What step can best help you to identify the specific needs and objectives of Country Fresh regarding privacy protection?

A. Assess Country Fresh's privacy maturity.
B. Review privacy laws and standards.
C. Identify the key stakeholders.
D. Physical audit of the facility.

110.   In analyzing Country Fresh's existing privacy program, you find procedures that are informal and incomplete. What stage does this represent in the AICPA/CICA Privacy Maturity Model?

A. Early.
B. Ad hoc.
C. Nonrepeatable.
D. Pre-program.

111.   Which of the following best describes who at Country Fresh needs to be trained on privacy protection?

A. Members of the privacy team, exclusively.
B. Department heads and key supervisors who can then train their personnel.
C. New hires only, as experienced employees should be familiar with the procedures.
D. Personnel in all departments who have any contact with personal data.

SCENARIO II
Use the following to answer questions 112-115:

A high-end United States retail firm that specializes in custom-made jewelry creates an opt-in program to provide personalized attention to its customers. On their first visit, customers are invited to log in to a kiosk in the retail store to enter their various shopping preferences, as well as personal information such as credit card numbers, banking information, birthdays, anniversary dates, etc. To make the customer experience even richer, the program also collects facial recognition data, so that when a customer enters the store, an alert staff member can call the customer by name and speak knowledgeably about his or her preferences, perhaps even directing the customer to a particular item. All the customer preference data, including facial recognition data, is encrypted, and stored on a computer system within the store. This computer system is also secured physically in a locked room.

Because the intent of this effort was benign, i.e., to enhance the overall customer experience, the owners of the retail store do not recognize that this collection of data has the potential to become a data privacy issue. No policies or procedures have been developed to address how this data is used or whether it can be resold. The owners simply assume that if a customer does not want to participate, they won't enter data into the kiosk.

An employee at the jewelry store, Matilda Jones, has full access to the data because she is the most computer-knowledgeable employee. Matilda has a friend who works for a wealth management firm in another U.S. state. Wishing to do her friend a business favor, she copies an unencrypted set of the customer names, preferences, and the facial recognition data onto a hard drive and sends it to her friend for him to use in marketing his wealth management services to preselected suitable customers. He intends to use the customer data in a way similar to the jewelers, to provide highly personalized service. Since she is not selling the data to him, Matilda does not think there is anything wrong with what she has done.

The owners of the wealth management company buy another list of customers and information legitimately from an outside vendor. This data includes financial information, as well as names, addresses, and number and brand of automobiles owned. The wealth management company collates the list with the list from the retailer, though the owners of the wealth management company are unaware the retailer's list was given informally, and now the wealth management firm has a very valuable list that contains a deep level of personal information about potential customers and their buying preferences.

The man who works at the wealth management firm puts the combined list up on an unencrypted public website so that Matilda can copy it back and enhance the jewelry store's original data set. While it is exposed, the wealth management company becomes the victim of an online attack, and the combined collection of customer data is stolen. The owners of the wealth management company only find this out when several of their customers report that their vehicles have been stolen. Further investigation of the crimes by the police links the data breach to home invasion burglaries. The criminals were using the stolen facial recognition data to identify potential victims, then using address data to find their primary residences. The owners of the retail jeweler have no knowledge any of this has happened until several months later, when the employee who traded their data to the wealth management firm quits and informs them of the data breach.

112. All of the following would protect the jewelry store's owners from future employee misuse of customer data EXCEPT:
A.   An updated privacy notice that reflects how customer data may be used.
B.   A notice to the wealth management customers about customer data mingling.
C.   An employment policy that calls for the removal of anyone who shares customer data.
D.   A better, policy-driven process for limiting access to customer data.

113.   After the breach is made known to the jewelry store, which task should it accomplish first?

A.   Coordinate with the wealth management company to limit the damage.
B.   Sue the wealth management company for the breach.
C.   Determine whether notification is legally required.
D.   Update its privacy notices to allow customers to opt out of the data use.

114.   After the data breach, what data can the wealth management company use legally?

A.   The combined data.
B.   Only the purchased data.
C.   None of the data.
D.   The original jewelry store's data.

115.   What would be the best way for the wealth management firm to respond to its customers' complaints?

A.   Assess the relative liabilities of all parties involved.
B.   Develop a formal opt-out procedure.
C.   Establish a formal complaint and resolution procedure.
D.   Create an ombudsman and refer complaints there.

Answer Key:

1. A	41. D	81. D.
2. D	42. D	82. B
3. B	43. A	83. D.
4. D	44. A	84. D.
5. B	45. D	85. D.
6. B	46. D	86. D.
7. B	47. B	87. D.
8. C	48. B	88. D
9. C	49. D	89. D
10. D	50. C	90. D
11. B	51. C	91. A
12. B	52. D	92. B
13. D	53. D	93. B
14. D	54. A	94. C
15. A	55. A	95. C
16. C	56. C	96. D
17. D	57. C	97. C
18. C	58. D	98. A
19. D	59. D	99. A
20. B	60. A	100. C
21. C	61. D	101. C
22. C	62. D	102. B
23. A	63. A	103. B
24. A	64. D	104. C
25. A	65. A	105. D
26. A	66. D	106. B
27. D	67. C	107. D
28. B	68. A	108. D
29. D	69. A	109. C
30. C	70. D	110. B
31. D	71. C	111. D
32. B	72. D	112. B
33. C	73. A	113. C
34. B	74. D	114. B
35. D	75. B	115. C
36. B	76. D	
37. D	77. C	
38. C	78. D	
39. D	79. D	
40. C	80. D	

Question 1.

One of the goals that is not a Privacy Program Manager role is to?

Answers:

A. To identify their supply chain's privacy risks.
B. To identify their organizations, employees, patient's risks.
C. To identify current state of policies, procedures, and any supporting documentation.
D. Promote consumer trust.

The correct answer is A. The PPM's goal is not to identify their supply chain's privacy risks. That would be a part of the Vendor Management program. Answer B and C are goals of the PPM. Answer D is a goal of the Privacy Program, which, ultimately, is an implied goal of the PPM. The best correct answer is A.

Question 2.

Which of the following is not a reason organization are becoming compliant with global privacy regulations?

Answers:

A. Brand Name Protection
B. Reputation Protection
C. GDPR
D. U.S. Federal Privacy Law

The correct answer is D. The U.S. has yet to pass and implement a federal privacy law. Sectors within the U.S. have passed federal laws that implicate data privacy protections, however, there is not a U.S. wide federal privacy law to date.

Question 3.

Privacy program managers are charged with the protection and appropriate use of?

Answers:

A. Private Information
B. Personal Information
C. Public Information
D. Social Information

The correct answer is B. The term Private Information is rarely utilized, while Personal Information (PI)and Personally Identifiable Information (PII) are predominantly used. PPMs are not responsible for protecting either public information or social information. Do not read into the questions. Focus on the question as it is posed. If you imply or apply additional thoughts to the question, you may over think the question and choose the incorrect answer.

Question 4.

Which of the following groups are not a priority group for the development of your privacy policies and procedures within your organization?

Answers:

A. Human Resources
B. Legal
C. Business Development
D. External Audit

The correct answer is D. An internal audit group would be a part of your priority group. All of the other groups are departments you should include.

Question 5.

The privacy vision should align with?

Answers:

A. Consumer Objectives
B. Business Objectives
C. Vendor Objectives
D. Contract Objectives

The correct answer is B. The privacy vision must support and align the business objectives to be successful.

Question 6.

Your organization is implementing a new process that may collect consumer's information. The process is complete and ready for a final review before being launched into production. During the review, it is determined that the new process lacks the ability to audit the privacy controls for regulatory compliance. What was not included in the design?

Answers:

A. Proactive
B. Embedded privacy controls
C. Respect for users
D. Privacy by Design

The correct answer is B. The PbD model supports and drives both privacy and security controls to be included in the design. As an embedded control, auditing the controls for regulatory compliance is correct. Ultimately, Answer A, C, and D are a part of the PbD model, however, the question explicitly identifies the lack of auditing capabilities, which is an embedded privacy control requirement.

Question 7.

Upon request, a detailed record of processing must be shared with the?

Answers:

A. Data Protection Officer
B. Data Protection Authority
C. Chief Information Officer
D. Chief Information Security Officer

The correct answer is B. Upon the request of the DPA, your organization must share the detailed record of processing with them. The other answers are also correct, however, the best, right answer is B. You will have questions like this on the exam.

Question 8.

Your medical staff has access to all EMRs. Each staff member is trained frequently on proper handling, access, and protecting of sensitive data. If one of your medical practitioners is unable to access an EMR, and is authorized to access it, which basic security principle has been applied?

Answers:

A. Role-Based Access
B. Segregation of duties
C. Least privilege
D. Need-to-know access

The correct answer is C. Least privilege access grants access to information or systems at the lowest level possible to perform their roles and responsibilities. In this scenario, the medical practitioner has not been provided access patient's record, therefore, must request it, based on least privilege access being applied.

Question 9.

While your organization is assessing a potential vendor, one statement within the vendor policy may require a review of?

Answers:

A. Privacy Policy
B. Vendor Management
C. Location of data
D. Employees

The correct answer is C. Knowing where your data will be located, stored, used, and shared is critical to an organization's data governance program. If your organization is restricted from sharing or transporting data to an inadequate country, you must know where the vendor processes your data.

Question 10.

Your organization has secured funding for a new privacy training initiative. Which of the following may not be one of the training methods you would implement?

Answers:

A. Classroom
B. Online
C. Workshops
D. Testing

The correct answer is D. However, pre-testing may be a way to baseline your workforce's knowledge of the training topic to better shape and deliver the actual training material for maximum comprehension.

Question 11.

The CFO and CHR of a healthcare organization are looking to you, the privacy program manager, to provide them with a performance measurement of the privacy program. Which of the following would you not utilize in creating that?

Answers:

A. Tracking
B. Identifying
C. Defining
D. Analyzing

The correct answer is B. The audience is already identified within the question. The other answers would all be utilized to create the performance measurement report.

Question 12.

Who needs to appreciate the benefits and risks associated with the collection and use of personal information?

Answers:

A. Privacy
B. Privacy Professional
C. Privacy Program Manager
D. Privacy Officer

The correct answer is B. Answers C and D are titles of professionals within Privacy.

Question 13.

A California, US based organization receives its first subject access request (SAR). The privacy program manager is alerted to receipt of the request in a timely fashion. What will the program manager reference, that was developed in the establishment of the privacy program, that will assist in determining where the SAR's information resides?

Answers:

A. Data Classification Policy
B. Privacy Program Scope
C. Regulatory Map
D. Data Inventory

The correct answer is D. The data inventory will provide the PPM with the source, types, uses, information flow path, storage, and other applicable data fields to start the collection of the SAR form.

Question 14.

The GDPR, the CCPA, GLBA and other privacy regulatory laws have different terminology and requirements as it relates to 'reasonable security procedures and practices." The word, "adequate" or "appropriate technical and organizational measures' – this is the 'security principle'. Where might you not reference for these types of controls and standards?

Answers:

A. Internet Security's Critical Security Controls
B. ISO/IEC 27002
C. NIST SP 800-53rev4
D. ISO/IEC 27006

The correct answer is D. ISO/IEC 27006 provides audit and certification for an ISMS and will not provide you the actual controls and standards to apply to particular data classifications and risks. Answers A, B, and C will provide you guidance for physical, administrative, and technical controls.

Question 15.

An organizations privacy program maturity level is based on how established the program is functioning in multiple areas. Departments are following and adhering to processes and procedures for most functions. What level of maturity is the organization at?

Answers:

A. Repeatable
B. Defined
C. Ad Hoc
D. Managed

The correct answer is A. Repeatable levels do have processes and procedures, however, there may still be gaps in complete documentation and lacking other areas of implementation.

Question 16.

An organizations privacy program maturity level is based on how established the program is functioning in multiple areas. Generally, if your privacy program has recently been created where you are still evaluating and inventorying what the organization has and does not have in place for policies, processes and procedures, the privacy program maturity level is at this stage?

Answers:

A. Repeatable
B. Defined
C. Ad Hoc
D. Managed

The correct answer is C. Ad Hoc levels are informal, incomplete and inconsistently implemented. It is the initial maturity level.

Question 17.

Key stakeholders make decisions pertaining your organizations privacy program. The record of these decisions serves as the privacy program's?

Answers:

A. Governance
B. Risk Assessment
C. Due Care
D. Due Diligence

The correct answer is D. GDPR requires organizations to keep a record of ownership, which supports the accountability requirements within the regulation. This particular question is looking at the functions and stakeholders who are accountable for privacy compliance.

Question 18.

Your customer's information and their rights to control what and who collects their information, where their information is shared are privacy rights. What overlap is there with information security that relates to accuracy of information?

Answers:

A. Availability
B. Confidentiality
C. Integrity
D. Accountability

The correct answer is C. Integrity is one of the information security triad's (C,I,A). Answers A and B are the other two security triads. Accountability does apply here, however, the question is asking about information security and how it relates to accuracy. Both integrity and accuracy ensure information is not altered in an unauthorized manner.

Question 19.

As privacy laws and regulations continue to expand and change, complying and monitoring with those changes is critical for the organization's privacy program success. What is one solution that provides organizations with updated changes, monitoring and auditing performances of their processes and procedures?

Answers:

A. Internal Audit
B. Second-party Audit
C. Third-party Audit
D. Third-party Privacy Compliance Platform and Tools

The correct answer is D. 3rd party external resources and tools provide organizations of any size with real-time legal and regulatory changes, particular audits and process compliance, along with baseline measures based on industry vertical and other criteria.

Question 20.

Prior to a new service or system being implemented, this type of action is required to be conducted?

Answers:

A. Data Privacy Impact Assessment
B. Privacy Impact Assessment
C. Privacy Assessment
D. Risk Assessment

The correct answer is B. Privacy Impact Assessment is and assessment of the privacy risks identified with processing of personal information in connection with a product, project or service. Answer A, Data Protection Impact Assessment must be conducted to identify risks when processing personal data and is required within the GDPR. Answer C, Privacy Assessment, measured an organization's compliance to legal and regulatory requirements, policies and processes and standards. Answer D, Risk Assessment, could be an assessment of any processes, that may or may not impact privacy or data protection.

Question 21.

Your organization has been alerted to a data breach within one of your vendors. During the DPA investigation, procurement has been summoned for questioning. What may be the topic of discussion?

Answers:

A. Communications Language
B. Processor responsibilities
C. GDPR Compliance
D. Internal audit results

The correct answer is C. DPA will investment reported data breaches and will look for GDPR compliance. That my consist of vendor assessments and contractual language (not Answer A). Answer B is not the correct answer for Procurement to respond to nor would Answer D.

Question 22.

Your organization is capturing and documenting where and what information is flowing, both internally and externally. What is this type of exercise?

Answers:

A. Regulatory Map
B. Legal Map
C. Data Inventory Map
D. Data Map

The correct answer is C. Answers A and B are to determine regulatory and legal requirements that your organization is accountable to and for. Answer D is the process of matching fields from one database to another.

Question 23.

Your organization is conducting processor assessments. Which privacy domain houses this action item?

Answers:

A. Measure
B. Improve
C. Evaluate
D. Support

The correct answer is A. Domains are: (A) Assess - Measure, (B) Protect - Improve, (C) Sustain - Evaluate or (D) Respond - Support.

Question 24.

HR is reviewing candidate's resumes and background information based on an open job posting. What is one risk area that you, as the Privacy Program Manager, should work with Legal and HR on, as it relates to the background information gathered?

Answers:

A. Data Retention
B. Data Policies
C. Information
D. Training

The correct answer is A. Data retention, not only at the controller's location, but also within the contract with the processor who is obtaining the background information. The controller must be explicit with what the processor will do with the information gathered on the individual once a decision has been executed on hiring or not hiring of the candidate. Based on that decision, both the controller and processor must retain and then destroy the data that is no longer required for any business reason.

Question 25.

Which of the following orders are the correct order as it relates to data incidents plans?

Answers:

A. Planning, Preparing, Handling, Reporting
B. Planning, Investigating, Handling, Reporting
C. Preparing, Reporting, Investigating, Recovering
D. Preparing, Investigating, Recovering, Reporting

The correct answer is A. Plan, Prepare, Roles and Responsibilities, Handling, Investigating, Reporting, and Recovery are the correct orders as it relates to data incidents.

Question 26.

Your customer's information and their rights to control what and who collects their information, where their information is shared are privacy rights. What overlap is there with information security that relates to access of information?

Answers:

A. Availability
B. Confidentiality
C. Integrity
D. Accountability

The correct answer is A. Availability is one of the information security triad's (C,I,A). Answers B and C are the other two security triads. Accountability does apply here, however, the question is asking about information security and how it relates to access. Both availability and access ensure information is available to authorized users.

Question 27.

Your medical staff has access to all EMRs. Each staff member is trained frequently on proper handling, access, and protecting of sensitive data. If one of your medical practitioners accesses an EMR in which they did not and will not provide care to, which basic security principle has been violated?

Answers:

A. Role-Based Access
B. Segregation of duties
C. Least privilege
D. Need-to-know access

The correct answer is D. Need-to-know access is access to information or systems that are required to conduct and complete the responsibility of an authorized user. In this scenario, the medical practitioner is not and will not provide care to the patient, therefore, has no need-to-know to access the patient's records.

Question 28.

Your PIA identified a risk that you, as the privacy program manager, must address to bridge a gap within your privacy training and awareness program. You present the findings and the costs associated with the mitigating activity to your leadership. They reject your request. What should you have presented to your leadership to support your request?

Answers:

A. Business Case
B. Return-on-Investment
C. Qualitative benefits
D. Annual loss expectancy (ALE)

The correct answer is B. Had an ROI and the savings (quantify vs qualitative) been presented along with the probable cost and impact that the risk may pose to the organization would have provided more strategic vision to the leadership vs. the bottom-line expenses. Answer A is incorrect, where the business case would have been created for the privacy program, which is already in place. Answer D would be utilized to quantify and support the ROI discussion.

Question 29.

A financial institution has completed their regulatory mapping exercise and determined and created their data retention policy. The institution has adopted two possible standards for destroying the data, which are degaussing and shredding. What is another way to destroy the data electronically?

Answers:

A. Melt
B. Burn
C. Erase
D. Overwrite

The correct answer is D. Answer A and B are physical, not electronic destruction methods. Answer C is a synonym for degaussing.

Question 30.

Your organization has suffered a data breach. You have initiated the incident response plan and are preparing for an external communication. Your marketing and social media team is made aware that an employee has posted a statement onto their personal social media platform. What didn't the organization do, based on the information provided?

Answers:

A. Implement a training program
B. Conduct training
C. Coordinate both internal and external communications
D. Notify customers

The correct answer is C. Coordinating both internal and external communications and then communicating those messages in sync will alleviate employees from posting inaccurate and unauthorized internal communications externally without specific guidance and provided templates, and reduction of confusion of anyone reading the communication of the employee.

Question 31.

Your organization has accepted your proposed privacy vision. In order to continue developing your privacy program, which is your next step?

Answers:

A. Develop the privacy team
B. Develop the privacy program strategy
C. Develop the mission statement
D. Develop the scope of the privacy program

The correct answer is D. After you have created and received approval of the vision or mission statement (C.), you must determine the scope of the privacy program. Answer A and B are subsequent steps after the vision/mission statement and scope have been established.

Question 32.

After completing the framework, which step is next in the development of the privacy program?

Answers:

A. Develop the privacy team
B. Develop the privacy program strategy
C. Develop the mission statement
D. Develop the scope of the privacy program

The correct answer is B. Once the vision/mission statement, scope and framework are selected, the strategy is next.

Question 33.

Which of the following tactics are used to identify your privacy program scope?

Answers:

A. Identify where business data is collected
B. Identify where data is collected
C. Identity where personal information is collected
D. Identify global data protection laws

The correct answer is C. You must know what personal information is collected and processed and which privacy and data protection laws and regulations impact your organization. Answer A is incorrect. You do not need to know, yet, what business data is collected, unless it is personal information. Answer B could be any data, that may not be personal data. Key words or the lack of key words is critical to catch during the exam.

Question 34.

Your organization has implemented information security practices. Which privacy domain houses this action item?

Answers:

A. Measure
B. Improve
C. Evaluate
D. Support

The correct answer is B. Domains are: (A) Assess - Measure, (B) Protect - Improve, (C) Sustain - Evaluate or (D) Respond - Support.

Question 35.

Your workforce is one of the key contributors to causing a data incident. What is one of the first things you need to determine to address this risk?

Answers:

A. Secure Funding
B. Train the workforce
C. Develop a business case
D. Workforce behavioral review

The correct answer is D. The disconnect between expected behavior and actual behavior is large. The organization needs to determine what the current behaviors are and then determine what are the desired behaviors. Once that is complete, the business case would then be created (Answer C) and presented to leadership to secure funding for the training (Answer A) and then execute the training (Answer B.)

Question 36.

HR is reviewing candidate's resumes and background information based on an open job posting. What is one risk area that you, as the Privacy Program Manager, should work focus on, as it relates to the vendor gathering the background information requested?

Answers:

A. Procurement
B. Vendor Assessment
C. Information Risk
D. Communications

The correct answer is B. The organization, prior to signing any contracts with a particular vendor, must assess the prospective vendor based on the organization's standards and regulatory requirements that must be complied with by the processor.

Question 37.

Your organization is implementing a new process that may collect consumer's information. Throughout the SDLC process, it is also determined that the consumer's information may be shared or aggregated throughout the life cycle of the information. In order to determine if a privacy impact assessment (PIA) is needed, you must conduct a?

Answers:

A. Data Privacy Impact Assessment
B. Information risk assessment
C. Privacy-enabling technology
D. Privacy threshold analysis

The correct answer is D. A DPIA is a tool which controllers provide proof and demonstrate compliance with data protection laws, which is not the correct answer here. PETs are utilized within the PbD model and not the correct answer here.

Question 38.

An insurance company is informed by an agent that they may have compromised personal information of their clients. What information security controls will be potentially implemented?

Answers:

A. Preventative
B. Detective
C. Corrective
D. Recovery

The correct answer is C. Corrective controls contain and minimize an incident from causing further damage. Answers A, B are implemented prior to an incident, while Answer D is implemented after the incident has been contained.

Question 39.

A U.S. based financial institution is required to provide customers a privacy notice annually that provides clear notice of the customer's right with respects to opt-outs. What regulation requires this?

Answers:

A. GDPR
B. LGDP
C. PIPEDA
D. GLBA

The correct answer is D. Answers A, B, and C are all international regulations, not U.S.

Question 40.

The stakeholders of a genetic organization have developed and are presenting their business case for a privacy program update, to include protective controls ensuring both the information security and privacy programs are united and overlapping. As part of this presentation, the quantified annual loss expectancy for a particular privacy control is $120,000 for complete development, implementation and monitoring of the control. While presenting, the question was posed to the presenter on, 'If the control is not implemented, what will be the cost to the organization?" The projected impact to the organization would be less than the actual control being implemented. What would this example be called?

Answers:

A. Qualitative model
B. Single loss expectancy
C. Return on investment (ROI)
D. Acceptable risk

The correct answer is C. ROI is (Benefits - Cost) / Cost. However, with this particular example, the risk is less than the actual proposed control and, depending on the difference between those costs (which was not provided deliberately), this may not be a good business case model to approve and implement if the ROI is not favorable, however, the question is only asking you what this example is called. Remember, do not add to the 'story' or question as you read it. Only read the answer (2x), call out the key words and determine what is being asked of you. Answer D could be the answer however, the actual question is not looking for that, but it looks and sounds good - a distracting answer. Answers A and B are incorrect.

Question 41.

An organizations privacy program maturity level is based on how established the program is functioning in multiple areas. The privacy program has been in place for multiple years and has been extremely successful in providing metrics and efficiencies for your organization. What level of maturity is the organization at?

Answers:

A. Repeatable
B. Defined
C. Ad Hoc
D. Managed

The correct answer is D. Managed maturity levels consist of reviews that assessed the effectiveness of the controls implemented.

Question 42.

Your medical staff has access to all EMRs. Each staff member is trained frequently on proper handling, access, and protecting of sensitive data. If one of your medical practitioners accesses an EMR in which they are providing care to, which basic security principle has been followed?

Answers:

A. Role-Based Access
B. Segregation of duties
C. Least privilege
D. Need-to-know access

The correct answer is D. Need-to-know access is access to information or systems that are required to conduct and complete the responsibility of an authorized user. In this scenario, the medical practitioner is authorized to access the patient's records.

Question 43.

As technology infrastructure is procured, implemented, and secured, which of the following security controls are most integrated with IT?

Answers:

A. Physical Security
B. HR Security
C. Ethics and Integrity
D. Employees

The correct answer is A. Systems and computers are physically protected and managed by doors and locks, CCTVs, etc. Answer B is integrated into IT; however, the question is asking about technology infrastructure (i.e. Computers, mobile devices, applications, etc.), therefore, the 'most' integrated with IT would be answer A.

Question 44.

Principles and standards, laws, regulations and programs are two categories that a privacy framework may be designed from. What is another category that can be referenced to create a privacy framework?

Answers:

A. Privacy Program Management
B. Privacy Program Strategy
C. Privacy Program Vision
D. Privacy by Default

The correct answer is A. Answer B and C are the foundation of the privacy program, however, are not frameworks. Answer D is a tricky answer. Privacy by design (PbD) would be a correct answer, however, 'default' is not the correct response.

Question 45.

Within the U.S., which federal law addresses money laundering?

Answers:

A. U.S. Federal Financial Law
B. Federal Trade Commission Act
C. Fair and Accurate Credit Transactions Act
D. Financial Modernization Act

The correct answer is D. Also known as the Gramm-Leach Bliley Act (GLBA) which requires financial institutions to explain how they share and protect their customer's private information.

Question 46.

Your organization must share personal information to a country outside of the EEA and EU. You individually tailor the contract your company's needs and obtain the required supervisory authority's authorization. What type of cross-border transfer rule are you using?

Answers:

A. BCR
B. SCC
C. Codes of Conduct
D. Ad hoc contractual clause

The correct answer is D. BCRs allow organization to create an internal policy. SCCs (Article 46(c) and Codes of conduct (Article 40) are addressed with the GDPR with enforceable commitments.

Question 47.

A global organization located in numerous countries would be best to implement this type of governance model?

Answers:

A. Centralized
B. Distributed
C. Hybrid
D. External

The correct answer is B. Distributed delegates decision-making to the lowest levels within an organization allowing a bottom-to-top flow of decisions and monitoring.

Question 48.

If your leadership is not supporting nor funding your privacy program management, one way to gain their support is to share what a potential privacy breach would cost the organizations. This would be an example of?

Answers:

A. Metrics
B. Quantitative Model
C. Qualitative Model
D. Return on Investment (ROI)

The correct answer is B. Showcasing exact costs (quantifiable numbers) generally assists privacy program managers in obtaining support and funding for their privacy program development.

Question 49.

What must an efficient and successful privacy program be built with?

Answers:

A. Data Map
B. Regulatory Map
C. Compliance Map
D. Comprehensive View

The correct answer is D. Answers A and B are components of the comprehensive view within the organization. Each organization must know what data that collect and process throughout the data's entire lifecycle.

Question 50.

Your organization completed the data inventory exercise. Who in your organization determines what classifications of information are arranged into those categories?

Answers:

A. Chief Security Officer
B. Chief Executive Officer
C. Privacy Officer
D. Human Resources

The correct answer is C. The Privacy Officer and legal department review all regulatory and legal requirements of the organization and based on those applicable laws, will determine what classifications will be utilized within the organization. Answer A will overlay the appropriate physical, administrative and technical controls, based on those categories of data. Answer B and D are not the correct answers.

Question 51.

Your organization has implemented a privacy program and you are analyzing the data and metrics. What was your previous step?

Answers:

A. Identification of audience
B. Analysis
C. Collection
D. Selection

The correct answer is C. The five-step metrics lifecycle Is: A. Identification of intended audiences B. Definition of data sources C. Selection of privacy metrics D. collection and Refinement of systems/application collecting points E. Analysis of the data/metrics

Question 52.

Once the policies, procedures and security controls have been assessed on your potential cloud provider, whom within your organization should approve of this type of vendor?

Answers:

A. General Counsel
B. Privacy Program Manager
C. Chief Information Security Officer
D. Chief Information Officer

The correct answer is D. All listed answers may be involved with the business case development, screening criteria of the vendor and review of the vendor, however, since it is a technical vendor, a cloud provider, ultimately, the CIO should approve of the provider.

Question 53.

Your organization is acquiring another organization. A part of the privacy checkpoint, your organization's processes should consist of conducting a _____ prior to the integration of the acquired organization's systems and processes.

Answers:

A. Divestiture
B. Data inventory
C. Regulatory map
D. Risk Assessment

The correct answer is D. A risk assessment of the acquired organization's systems, processes, and technologies should be conducted prior to integrating systems to your organization's systems. This will identify potential risks and allow time to mitigate those while protecting and not introducing those new risks to your organization.

Question 54.

The privacy program manager is preparing their performance measurement presentation. They are looking at the value of the asset being measured, ensuring to capture the possible changes or factors that may impact that value. What other consideration should the PPM take into account as they develop the presentation?

Answers:

A. Return on investment
B. Chief Financial Officer
C. Alignment
D. Integration

The correct answer is A. The PPM must ensure that the ROI is connected and justifies the implementation of that particular function. Answers C and D are not the correct terms for use in a performance measurement analysis.

Question 55.

An insurance company is informed by an agent noticed that their computer screen is open, and they are certain that they had locked the screen and that they may have compromised personal information of their clients. What information security controls may be audited?

Answers:

A. Access Controls
B. Asset Management
C. Procurement
D. Training

The correct answer is A. Access controls may be audited to see who accessed the computer, when, and what was accessed.

Question 56.

You are making a purchase on an e-commerce website and you receive a notice in the middle of the page that articulates what the organization does to protect your information. You have not yet provided any personal information. What is this called?

Answers:

A. Opt-Out
B. Opt-In
C. Just-in-time-notice
D. Privacy Policy

The correct answer is C. The notice is provided to the customer before any information is collected and articulates how that information will protected along with the consumer's choices and rights. It is an external statement. A privacy policy is an internal communication.

Question 57.

An organizations privacy program maturity level is based on how established the program is functioning in multiple areas. Regular audits, assessments, guidance and communications are gathered to review and improve the overall privacy program. What level of maturity is the organization at?

Answers:

A. Repeatable
B. Defined
C. Optimized
D. Managed

The correct answer is C. Optimized level provides reviews, communications and improvements for the program.

Question 58.

Your customer's information and their rights to control what and who collects their information, where their information is shared are privacy rights. What overlap is there with information security that relates to accountability?

Answers:

A. Availability
B. Confidentiality
C. Integrity
D. Accountability

The correct answer is D. Answers A, B and C are the information security triads. Accountability falls in both privacy and information security requiring data owners, controllers, and processors to protect the data adequately.

Question 59.

It is Monday morning and you are starting a new role. You log into your corporate email account and find an email from HR. As you read through the email, you see that you are required to complete specific privacy training. What type of control is this?

A. Special Handling
B. Data Classification
C. Technical
D. Role-Based Access

The correct answer is D. You are starting a new role; you are being required to complete 'specific' privacy training. Answer A, B, and C will support Role-Based Access controls, but are not the correct answers here.

Question 60.

HR is reviewing candidate's resumes and background information based on an open job posting. What is one risk area that you, as the Privacy Program Manager, should work with HR on, as it relates to the background information gathered?

Answers:

A. Contracts
B. Procurement
C. Marketing
D. Data

The correct answer is A. Contracts and explicit requirements of processers that gather background information on behalf of the hiring organization. Answer B and C are not correct. Answer D, based on the actual question, is a distracting answer and the incorrect answer.

Question 61.

Your organization has suffered a data breach. Your organization has implemented their incident response plan. Which privacy domain houses this action item?

Answers:

A. Measure
B. Improve
C. Evaluate
D. Support

The correct answer is D. Domains are: (A) Assess - Measure, (B) Protect - Improve, (C) Sustain - Evaluate or (D) Respond - Support.

Question 62.

Your privacy program needs to monitor changes, organizational compliance, but it doesn't need to integrate with?

Answers:

A. Legal changes
B. Cultural changes
C. Technological changes
D. Employee changes

The correct answer is D. Although employee changes are important to understand and take into consideration, as it relates to the privacy program, employee changes are not a priority. Cultural changes (answer B) are a priority to take into consideration as a whole, but not the individual employee changes.

Question 63.

Your organization has implemented a privacy program and you are preparing to present metrics captured. What was your initial step in this process?

Answers:

A. Identification of audience
B. Analysis
C. Collection
D. Selection

The correct answer is A. The five-step metrics lifecycle Is: A. Identification of intended audiences B. Definition of data sources C. Selection of privacy metrics D. collection and Refinement of systems/application collecting points E. Analysis of the data/metrics

Question 64.

Your organization has implemented a privacy program and you are defining your data sources. What is your next step?

Answers:

A. Identification of audience
B. Analysis
C. Collection
D. Selection

The correct answer is D. The five-step metrics lifecycle Is: A. Identification of intended audiences B. Definition of data sources C. Selection of privacy metrics D. collection and Refinement of systems/application collecting points E. Analysis of the data/metrics

Question 65.

An insurance company is informed by an agent that they may have compromised personal information of their clients. What is this called when the agent thinks the information has been compromised?

Answers:

A. Incident Detection
B. Incident Handling
C. Incident Response Plan
D. Employee Training

The correct answer is A. The presumption of this question, which you will see similar questions on your exam, states that an agent has informed the organization that they may have an incident. They detected something and notified. This also implies that the organization has already trained (Answer D) the employee on the IRP (Answer C) which is a part of the handling of the incident (Answer B). Understanding Incident Response is critical.

Question 66.

When your organization has purchased cyber liability insurance, and suffer a data breach, your incident response plan is then followed and one of the first calls would be to?

Answers:

A. Forensic Firm
B. Data Protection Authority
C. CSO
D. Breach Coach

The correct answer is D. The breach coach is an outside legal firm/counsel that will assist in triaging and providing the organization with legal guidance vs. in-house legal team providing 'business' guidance. Answer A would be contacted after and directly from the breach coach, which provides the organization with privileged rights.

Question 67.

Who, within your organization, would the privacy program manager not work with to better understand the organizations privacy needs?

Answers:

A. CPO
B. DPO
C. DPA
D. General Counsel

The correct answer is C. The DPA will not provide the PPM with privacy insights within their organization. They may provide templates and guidance on how to learn of those, however. The other answers are primary functional leaders that would provide great insight to the privacy needs of your organization.

Question 68.

Of the following, which is a privacy framework that may be used for your privacy program management framework?

Answers:

A. ENISA
B. EFCC
C. CNIL
D. DPA

The correct answer is A. The European Union Agency for Network and Information Security (ENISA) is a possible privacy program management framework. The others all sound good but are not correct.

Question 69.

This regulation offers organizations a new framework for data protection?

Answers:

A. GDPR
B. LGDP
C. PIPEDA
D. APPI

The correct answer is A. GDPR also requires organizations to be accountable with global impacts. LGDP is the newly approved Brazilian General Data Protection Law. PIPEDA applies to Canada and APPI applies to Japan's Act on Protection of Personal Information.

Question 70.

As you assess your prospective vendors, what is one topic that is not a priority for you to assess?

Answers:

A. Financial
B. Geographic Location(s)
C. Privacy Framework
D. Data Inventory

The correct answer is D. Yes, you need a data inventory and will add to it once you add vendors to your vendor management portfolio, but as a prospective vendor, you do not need to focus on that, yet.

Question 71.

You are making a purchase on an e-commerce website and a banner at the bottom of the page appears before you can provide your billing and shipping information. This banner articulates what the organization does to protect your information. What is this called?

Answers:

A. Opt-Out
B. Opt-In
C. Privacy Notice
D. Privacy Policy

The correct answer is C. The statement is a promise to the consumer on what information is collected, how it will be protected, and the consumer's choices and rights. It is an external statement. A privacy policy is an internal communication.

Question 72.

What is measured via metrics associated with confidentiality, unavailability, and projected business impact assessments for downtime within an organizations business objectives?

Answers:

A. Accountability
B. Data Privacy
C. Data Protection
D. Business Resiliency

The correct answer is D. The BIA will provide quantitative values and expenses if unavailable and will drive the DR and BCP to protect and defend your business operations if an outage was to be realized, which is business resiliency. Answers A, B, and C are all incorrect.

Question 73.

A California, U.S. based organization receives its first subject access request (SAR). The privacy program manager is alerted to receipt of the request in a timely fashion. What is the first step of the organization upon receipt of the SAR?

Answers:

A. Verify Identity of Requestor
B. Review BIPA
C. Regulatory Map
D. Data Inventory

The correct answer is A. Verification of the requestor is required prior to any next steps, to ensure personal data is protected, and that the confidentiality, integrity and availability are protected. Any data subject-access requests made by unauthorized persons and the SAR is provided to that unauthorized person, will result in a breach.

Question 74.

Which of the following are not privacy matters to consider?

Answers:

A. Geographical location
B. Global Privacy Regulations
C. Cross-border data sharing
D. Competitor's Privacy Strategy

The correct answer is D. Although it would be nice to know what your competitors are doing, it is not a priority for your privacy program to focus on. The other three answers are and should be taken into consideration.

Question 75.

What is developed to guide your organization in disseminating and adoption for your privacy program?

Answers:

A. Developing the privacy vision
B. Developing the privacy strategy
C. Developing the privacy framework
D. Developing the privacy structure

The correct answer is B. The vision won't guide your organizations' communications or your leadership's adoption for the PPM. Answers C and D are possible answers but won't be a driver for adoption for your PPM.

Question 76.

Within your organization, who is responsible for protecting personal information that is captured and processed?

Answers:

A. Consumer
B. Vendor
C. Patient
D. Workforce

The correct answer is D. The key words are, "Within your organization", which then nullifies the Consumer, Vendor, and Patient answers.

Question 77.

What must be implemented and is the first cornerstone that builds a foundation for an effective privacy management program?

Answers:

A. Privacy Vision
B. Privacy Scope
C. Privacy Framework
D. Privacy Strategy

The correct answer is C. The framework is the critical to protecting the privacy of your organization's data and is the foundation for an effective privacy program.

Question 78.

Your organization is capturing and documenting where and what information is flowing, both internally and externally. What does the end product assist your organization with?

Answers:

A. Identifies vendors
B. Identifies regulatory requirements
C. Identifies classification
D. Identifies personal information use

The correct answer is D. A data inventory will identify the source, types and uses of personal information. Answer A and B could be an answer, but not with the limited information provided. Answer C would be a by-product of the identification of the personal use information.

Question 79.

Your organization, a covered entity within the U.S., has suffered a data breach within your archived information. What policy will be looked at to determine whether or not your organization has complied with that policy?

Answers:

A. Acceptable Use
B. BYOD
C. Incident Response Plan
D. Retention

The correct answer is D. The key word in the question is 'archived', meaning stored and leading to the review of your retention of information.

Question 80.

Your organization is structuring your privacy team. Which privacy domain houses this action item?

Answers:

A. Measure
B. Improve
C. Privacy Program Framework
D. Developing a Privacy Program

The correct answer is D. When your organization is developing the privacy program, they will create the company vision, establish a data governance model, establish a privacy program, structure the privacy team and communicate, both internally and externally pertaining to their accountability.

Question 81.

Under what U.S. law requires government agencies to conduct a privacy impact assessment?

Answers:

A. FISMA
B. FACTA
C. E-Commerce Act
D. E-Government Act

The correct answer is D. The key word is 'government'. If you caught that, you answered the question correctly.

Question 82.

An insurance company is informed by an agent that they may have compromised personal information of their clients. What is this called?

Answers:

A. Data Breach
B. Privacy Incident
C. Cyber Security
D. Incident Response Framework

The correct answer is B. The key word is 'may' have compromised. It has not been confirmed or validated, so, at this point, it is unknown if it is a data breach. Remember, you can have an incident without a data breach, but you cannot have a data breach without an incident.

Question 83.

Who is responsible for monitoring, improving, reporting and communicating the criticality of a particular metric?

Answers:

A. Privacy Manager
B. Privacy Owner
C. Communications Leader
D. Metric owner

The correct answer is D. They must be able to communicate the value and purpose of the metric to the organization.

Question 84.

An international manufacturing company is implementing their privacy program. While they are in that process, they are conducting self-assessments, developing procedures, communicating and monitoring the program. What type of management is this called?

Answers:

A. Information Security Management System
B. Risk Management
C. Centralized Management
D. Information Management

The correct answer is D. Answer A is a security management system. Answer B is incorrect. Answer C is a governance model. Information management consists of discovering, building, communicating, and growth.

Question 85.

Your organization has suffered a data breach. You have initiated the incident response plan and are preparing for an external communication. Which or who would be best to communicate that message externally?

Answers:

A. HR
B. Ethics and Integrity
C. Marketing Dept.
D. CEO

The correct answer is D. Answer A is the voice to the employees, internally. Answer B is not correct. Answer C may work with the PR/Communications group on the message; however, Answer D is best and recommended to communicate externally.

Question 86.

In order for you to assess a cloud provider, you must understand their?

Answers:

A. Privacy
B. Mission Statement
C. Notice
D. Policies

The correct answer is D. Their mission statement (answer B) is something to view and will support their policies, which will help you assess the cloud provider. Answer A and C are not relevant to this particular question.

Question 87.

Which one of the following is not one of the most common causes of a data breach?

Answers:

A. Malicious Actors
B. Human Error
C. System Glitches
D. Vendors

The correct answer is D. The top three causes are answers A, B, and C. Vendors are up there, but not the most common cause.

Question 88.

The information security group utilizes a systematic approach to manage information risks relating to people, processes, and technologies. What is the name of this approach?

Answers:

A. Privacy Framework
B. Information Security
C. Information Privacy Management System
D. Information Security Management System

The correct answer is D. ISO/IEC 27000 Information Security Management System (ISMS) series provides an overview and guidance to what and how to implement an ISMS.

Question 89.

These guidelines apply to all media and address marketing plans?

Answers:

A. Network Advertising Initiative (NAI)
B. VeriSign
C. PCI DSS
D. DMA Guidelines for Ethical Business Practices

The correct answer is D. NAI is an an industry trade group that develops self-regulatory standards for online advertising. VeriSign enables the security, stability and resiliency of key internet infrastructure and services, including the .com and .net domains. PCI DSS is the information security standard for organizations that handle branded credit cards from the major card schemes.

Question 90.

Privacy programs and their leadership may fall under multiple areas within organizations. They may fall under Legal, HR, IT, Risk, or other areas.
As your organization determines which area it may report to, the organization should take all of the following into consideration, except:

Answers:

112.   Organizational structure
113.   Roles and responsibilities
114.   Evaluation
115.   Vendor Management

The correct answer is D. All of the other answers should be taken into consideration as the organization determines where the program and its leaders will fall under.

Printed in Great Britain
by Amazon